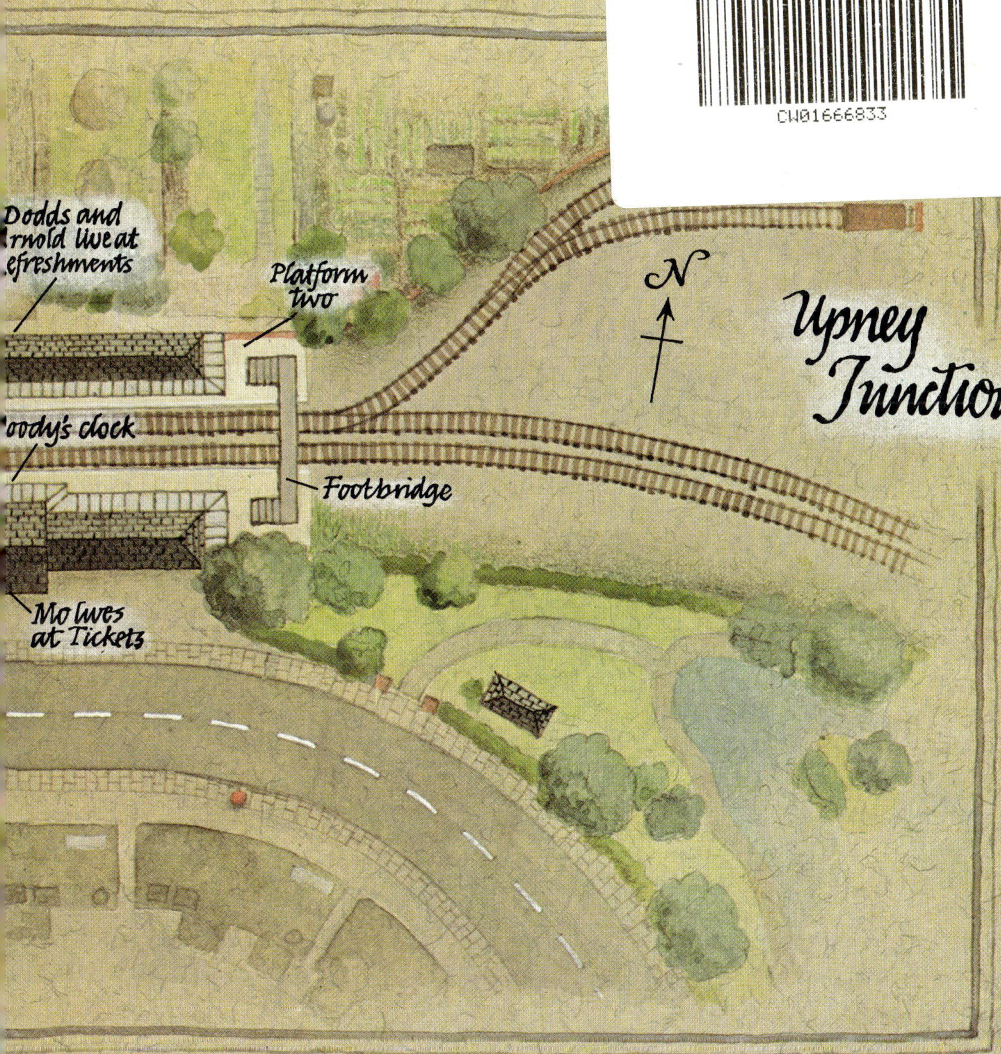

Ben :- 29th April 1986

Mick, Maurice and Bernard – thanks!

First published 1983 by Macdonald & Co (Publishers) Ltd, Maxwell House, 74 Worship St, London, EC2A 2EN
 ISBN 0 356 09185 6
Printed and bound by Purnell & Sons (Book Production) Ltd, Paulton, England

NICK BUTTERWORTH

INVASION AT UPNEY JUNCTION

MACDONALD

Mo the mouse was restless. For the last three nights he had been troubled by strange noises in the middle of the night. But he couldn't tell whether or not he had been dreaming.

'I shall have to speak to Murdoch about it next time I see him,' yawned Mo, sleepily opening one eye. But even as he spoke, there came a knock at his door and Murdoch the toad stuck his head in.

'Morning Mo,' he croaked. 'You still in bed?'

'Come in Murdoch,' said Mo. 'Yes, I've been having the weirdest dreams. Full of bangs and thumps and cackling laughter. What do you make of it?'

'I'd say you should lay off the late night Gorgonzola,' replied Murdoch, 'except that I've heard noises echoing around the drains. And the air down there has become all musty and fusty.'

Just then, there was another knock at the door.

'Anybody home?'

'Hi Woody,' said Mo. 'Hey! You might have wiped your feet! Look at these muddy footprints!'

'They're not mine,' protested Woody.

'Nor mine,' added Murdoch. 'But look – they're everywhere.'

'And there's newspaper strewn all over the place,' said Woody. The three friends looked puzzled.

Meanwhile at Refreshments, Dodds and Arnold had made another strange discovery. Their store of digestive biscuits had mysteriously vanished.

'I reckon you've been sleep-eating again,' said Arnold.

'Not a whole packet!' said Dodds.

'Oh well,' said Arnold, 'let's see if we can scrounge breakfast at Tickets with Mo. Come on.' The two set out across the station.

'Where on earth has all this rubbish come from?' said Arnold. 'Look at the mess.'

At Tickets they found the others and joined in the discussion. But it wasn't long before they were loudly interrupted by the arrival of Theo.

'All right!' he bellowed, 'who thinks it's funny to rip a chap's newspaper to shreds?'

'Hold your horses, Theo,' said Murdoch. 'It wasn't anybody here.'

'But what *is* going on?' said Woody. 'Banging and cackling in the night. Fusty smells, disappearing food, and poor Theo's paper?' Mo looked serious.

'I smell a rat,' he said.

'Do you indeed?' said a cold voice. 'It seems, my friend, that you have a keen nose.'

Mo spun round and to his horror saw not one, but three huge rats towering in the doorway. The one in the middle looked at the other two.

'Perhaps one of us is not being careful enough about personal freshness,' it leered. They fell about cackling and then, without being asked, strode right into Mo's house and looked around.

'This'll do nicely for our HQ,' said their leader. 'We're taking over the station. Scram.'

Mo was quaking inside.

'Look here,' he said angrily, 'you can't just walk in here like you owned the place.'

'Oh yeah?' said the rat. 'And what do you think five puny mice and one fat toad can do about it?'

'This!' yelled Murdoch. To everyone's amazement, he sprang high into the air and landed with a thump on top of the biggest rat. Dodds put his head down and, like a battering ram, ran to hit one of the rats hard below the belt. Mo and Woody brought down the third rat with a combined rugby tackle. Arnold finished him off by bouncing Mo's favourite mug off the top of the rat's head! Even Theo joined in by sinking his sharp teeth into the chief rat's tail.

'Keep it up, lads,' cried Mo, 'we're winning.' But at that moment there was a scuffling at the door and six more rats burst into Tickets and joined the battle.

It was all too much. Five mice and a toad were no match for nine enormous rats all kicking, biting and scratching.

'Sound the retreat!' cried Mo. The *Battle of Tickets* had been lost! Mo led the friends to a secret hideout in an old oildrum which lay on a rubbish dump at the end of Platform One. They struggled into the drum through a hole in one end and slumped onto the floor, battered and exhausted. Eventually Woody spoke.

'Round one to the rats,' he said. Mo nodded slowly and frowned. Then turning to Murdoch he said,

'That was tremendous when you jumped on that chief rat! Where did you learn to leap like that?'

'Ah,' grunted Murdoch, 'little trick my cousin taught me. He's a frog.'

'Anybody hurt?' asked Woody. Everybody seemed to be all right – apart from Dodds who had a headache.

'How about you Theo. . . ' Woody stopped. 'Hey – where's Theo? He's not here!'

'Shhh! What's that?' said Mo suddenly. He peered through a split in the drum. 'Rats!' he whispered. They all listened. Sure enough, two voices could be heard in conversation outside the drum.

'We should never have let 'em escape like that,' said one rat.

'You worry too much, Sidney,' replied the other. 'What can they do? Anyway that old codger will tell us where to find them. Then we'll finish the job.'

As soon as the rats had gone the mice in the oildrum began to talk excitedly.

'They've got Theo!' squealed Arnold. 'We must rescue him!'

'Yes,' said Mo, 'but we must wait until it's dark. We've got to be careful. We don't even know where they're holding him.'

'If I know rats,' said Murdoch, 'there'll be a wild party tonight. They'll be at Refreshments.'

Murdoch was right. Already the rats were celebrating their victory and making a terrible rumpus over at Refreshments. And in the middle of it all, bound and gagged, being prodded and jeered at, was poor Theo!

As soon as it grew dark Mo called his friends together.

'The rats are probably holding Theo at your place, Dodds,' said Mo, 'so you'd better come with Woody and me.'

'It's my place too,' said Arnold.

'But the fewer the better,' said Mo, 'and we might need Dodds' strength.'

'Arnold and I will guard the hideout,' said Murdoch. This seemed to satisfy Arnold.

The station clock said 8.32 precisely as Mo, Woody and Dodds set off to Refreshments.

'Remember,' said Mo, 'we'll need to be as quiet as mice.'

'We are mice,' said Dodds, looking puzzled.

'Exactly,' said Mo.

'I know a secret way in through the air vent,' said Dodds.

'Lead on,' whispered Mo. As they squeezed through the vent, they could hardly believe the awful sight which lay before them: torn boxes and empty food packets strewn all over the place. And in the middle of it all, the sleeping, snoring bodies of nine fat rats! The three mice tiptoed past the rubbish and the rats in search of Theo.

'Yech!' said Woody. 'What a pong!'

'Sshh!' whispered Dodds loudly, and promptly tripped over a rat's tail and fell with a thud. Mo looked anxiously at the rat, but it just let out a loud snore, smiling stupidly.

Suddenly they heard a strange noise.

'Mmm mmm! Mmmm!'

'Look!' said Woody, pointing. 'It's Theo!'

Poor Theo. The rats had tied him to the leg of a chair and gagged him with his own scarf. In no time at all they set him free and then escorted him stealthily back across the dark station to their hideout.

'Thank goodness you came,' said Theo. 'They were planning to hunt you down first thing tomorrow, and finish us all off!'

'Well, we're safe for the moment,' said Mo. 'But we can't live in an oildrum and just leave our homes to the rats. We've got to find a way to get rid of them for good. Let's sleep on it.'

Mo was up at the crack of dawn. He didn't take kindly to being exiled by a bunch of rats. He hadn't slept. Instead he had lain awake, plotting his revenge. And he had had an idea, a beautiful idea, if only it would work! At first light, he slipped out of the oildrum hideout and made a careful inspection of the rubbish dump. Yes. It might just work! He returned to his friends.

By now everyone was stirring.

'You're looking pleased with yourself,' said Theo as Mo entered. Mo grinned.

'Do you think those rats could get through the door to our hideout?' he asked. Theo turned to Mo, frowning.

'It's very worrying,' he replied, 'but I think they could.'

'Good, good,' said Mo. The others looked blank. 'Next question. Who holds the record for wood-gnawing?' Everyone agreed that Woody was the champion.

'Right. Come with me.' Mystified, they all followed Mo to a part of the dump where the oildrum rested against an old chair-leg. Mo explained that he wanted it whittled down till it was ready to break.

'Should be a piece of cake,' replied Woody.

'Go to it,' said Mo. 'Then find a long piece of string and tie it to the top.' None the wiser, Woody set to work.

1

'Come on,' said Mo to Murdoch and Dodds. He led them to the hole in the end of the oildrum and pointed to a hinged cap above it. 'Could you two reach that and close it?'

Murdoch and Dodds reached up and pulled. The cap was rusty but it offered no resistance to a large mouse and a fat toad. It squeaked and snapped shut.

'One last thing,' said Mo, leading them all back into the oildrum. At the far end there was a split in the rim. Watched by his puzzled friends, Mo squeezed through to the outside and then squeezed back.

'Perfect!' he said.

'What's all this about?' asked Arnold impatiently. Mo cleared his throat.

'Gather round everybody. Here's the plan.' He explained what he wanted each of his friends to do. 'Is everybody clear?' They all nodded. 'Good; I'm off to find those rats.'

Mo didn't have far to look. He could hear harsh voices laughing and jeering up ahead.

'It's now or never,' he said to himself, and sticking his head round a corner, came face to face with the rats.

'Well, well,' said Mo. 'It's you lot. I thought it was a rotten cabbage rolling up the platform!'

For an instant the rats were speechless. Then with shouts and yells they chased after Mo.

'Should have given this part of the plan to Woody!' thought Mo as he shot up the length of Platform One. He led the shouting rabble towards the oildrum. He only hoped that his friends had remembered their part of the plan.

'You lot couldn't catch a cold!' Mo jeered as he darted into the oildrum. The rats rushed in after him. Cursing and bellowing in the darkness, none of them saw Mo squeeze through the small hole in the other end of the drum.

'Action stations!' yelled Murdoch. He and Dodds sprang out of hiding and using all their strength, closed the oildrum's rusty cap. Woody, Arnold and Theo pulled on their string, the old chair-leg broke and the drum started to move! With howls of dismay from the rats inside, it rumbled down the rubbish dump, gathering speed. Then, it clattered onto the railway lines rolling faster and faster along the tracks, until it was just a speck in the distance! They watched it disappear.

'Come on,' said Dodds, as they wandered back up the platform, 'we've got a lot of cleaning up to do at Refreshments.'

'Rats!' said Arnold.

VERY STEEP
LEVEL

Woody

Mo

Theo